Pope John Paul II on

THE
GENIUS
OF
WOMEN

Pope John Paul II on The Genius of Women was a project of the bishops' Committee on Women in Society and in the Church. It was approved for publication by the Administrative Committee in March 1997 and is authorized for publication by the undersigned.

Monsignor Dennis M. Schnurr
General Secretary
NCCB/USCC

ISBN 1-57455-113-2
First Printing, August 1997

Contents

The Church Prepares for the UN Conference on Women: A Compilation of Papal Statements

Excerpts of Related Interest from Other 1995 Papal Statements

Foreword

This compilation, *The Genius of Women,* * focuses on 1995—a truly memorable year for women in the Catholic Church—and includes major papal statements issued during that year to and about women.

These statements, remarkable though they are, follow in a line of church documents that highlight women and their concerns. The Second Vatican Council generated intense interest in many aspects of church life, including the situation of women. Major church documents began to appear that took note of the emerging pastoral concerns around women. Here are a few examples.

Gaudium et Spes, Vatican II's *Constitution on the Church in the Modern World*, reaffirmed the basic equality of all people: "All women and men are endowed with a rational soul and are created in God's image; . . . there is here a basic equality between all and it must be accorded ever greater recognition. . . . [A]ny kind of social or cultural discrimination in basic personal rights on the grounds of sex, race, color, social conditions, language, or religion, must be curbed and eradicated as incompatible with God's design. It is deeply to be deplored that these basic personal rights are not yet being respected everywhere, as is the case with women who are

*The phrase "the genius of women" appears frequently in the writings of Pope John Paul II. Although the word *genius* has several meanings, the pope uses it to connote *an essential nature or spirit.*

denied the chance freely to choose a husband, or a state of life, or to have access to the same educational and cultural benefits as are available to men" (no. 29).

Later, *Gaudium et Spes* emphasizes that "At present women are involved in nearly all spheres of life: they ought to be permitted to play their part fully in ways suited to their nature. It is up to everyone to see to it that women's specific and necessary participation in cultural life be acknowledged and developed" (no. 60).

The Synod on the Vocation and Mission of the Laity, held in 1987, occasioned two landmark papal documents on women. The first, *Mulieris Dignitatem* (1988), was called a "meditation" on women by Pope John Paul II. Beginning with Genesis, the pope prayerfully considers the consequences of the Creator's decision that the human being should always exist as a woman or a man. Moving through Scripture, the meditation probes the mystery at the heart of human life: that we are made in God's image, as we are, men and women. Mary, the mother of Jesus, and the many women in the life of Jesus and in the life of the Church are presented as icons—windows to the mysteries of the Triune God. The meditation concludes: "The Church gives thanks *for all the manifestations of the feminine 'genius'* which have appeared in the course of history, in the midst of all peoples and nations; . . . She gives thanks for all the *fruits of feminine holiness*" (no. 31).

In *Mulieris Dignitatem* the pope sets out the anthropological and theological foundation regarding the dignity and significance of women and men. It is, therefore, a key document to understanding his subsequent writings on women. Because this volume is limited to 1995, *Mulieris Dignitatem* is not reproduced here, but readers are encouraged to read the text in its entirety.

Several months later, the apostolic exhortation on the laity, *Christifideles Laici*, appeared. The exhortation repeats the Synod's invitation "to once again acknowledge the indispensable contribution of women to the building up of the Church and the development of society." Women's personal dignity must be affirmed; this is the first step in promoting the full participation of women in the Church and in society. Perhaps most important, however, are these lines: "It is necessary that the Church recognize all the gifts of men and women for her life and mission, and put them into practice" (no. 49).

The activities of the National Conference of Catholic Bishops have also reflected this concern for women. In 1983, the NCCB began a nearly decade-long attempt to write a pastoral letter on women. This effort, although unsuccessful, did produce a list of twenty-five recommendations for action. Some of these recommendations have already been implemented, including a strong statement by the U.S. bishops against domestic violence (*When I Call for Help*) and a pastoral plan for ministry with young adults (*Sons and Daughters of the Light*), which discusses the importance of marriage preparation for young couples as well as the special needs of single young adults.

In 1994, the Congregation for the Doctrine of the Faith issued *Ordinatio Sacerdotalis*, reaffirming that priestly ordination is restricted to men. This inspired the bishops' pastoral reflection, *Strengthening the Bonds of Peace* (1995), which considers women's leadership, the equality of women and men, and the diversity of women's gifts and talents. *Strengthening the Bonds of Peace* calls for an ongoing dialogue between women and men in the Church and pledges the bishops to continue the dialogue "in a spirit of partnership and mutual trust." Subsequently, the NCCB Secretariat for Family, Laity, Women and Youth developed a parish resource packet to help promote a dialogue on the local level.

By the end of 1994, the stage had been set for the Church to focus even more intensely on women. The foundations had been laid, the broad themes enunciated, and the Church's "Year of the Woman" was about to begin.

Introduction

As 1995 opened, countries and nongovernmental organizations around the world were preparing for the United Nations Fourth World Conference on Women, to be held in Beijing in September. With global attention focused on women, Pope John Paul II took the opportunity to speak out on women's behalf. Beginning with his World Day of Peace Message on January 1, and continuing with a series of Angelus reflections and the *Letter to Women*, the Holy Father repeatedly affirmed women's gifts and leadership and praised the "genius of women."

The bishops' Committee on Women in Society and in the Church recognized the significance of these statements and brought them together in this compendium. Wherever possible the entire text has been reprinted; however, where excerpts appear, they are accompanied by a full citation so readers can obtain the complete text. The committee compiled these statements to make them more accessible to lay women and men, clergy, and religious who seek to deepen their understanding of the changing role of women in the Church and in society. The committee invites women and men to read these statements thoughtfully, to reflect on them prayerfully, and to consider their practical application. In particular, it urges that local churches use this compendium as they prepare to celebrate the Third Millennium.

The compendium can be a helpful resource to dioceses, parishes, and lay movements and organizations. Parishes, for example, might use it with their pastoral councils, with post-RENEW or similar groups, or as part of their adult education programs. Dioceses could feature it in their continuing education for priests. Seminaries might use it as a reference work and for assigned reading in courses or workshops. The statements can provide a common ground for fruitful discussions about women and their participation in Church and society.

One consistent theme unites these papal texts: they all invite committed action on behalf of women. This compendium strives to enable both the dialogue and the action to go forward. Reflecting on the Holy Father's words, we can indeed answer his challenge "to move from words to deeds" as we stand on the threshold of the new millennium.

THE CHURCH
PREPARES FOR THE
UN CONFERENCE
ON WOMEN: A
COMPILATION OF
PAPAL STATEMENTS

World Day of Peace Message

The Holy Father's World Day of Peace Message *invites women "to become teachers of peace with their whole being and in all their actions." His message anticipates many of the key themes of the Beijing Conference: promoting women's dignity in a world that often exploits women, discrimination against female children, and women as victims of violence. The complete text follows.*

January 1, 1995

1. At the beginning of 1995, with my gaze fixed on the new millennium now fast approaching, I once again address to you, men and women of good will, a pressing appeal for peace in the world.

The violence which so many individuals and peoples continue to experience, the wars which still cause bloodshed in many areas of the world and the injustice which burdens the life of whole continents can no longer be tolerated.

The time has come to move from words to deeds: May individual citizens and families, believers and churches, states and international organizations all recognize that they are called to renew their commitment to work for peace!

Everyone is aware of the difficulty of this task. If it is to be effective and long lasting, work for peace cannot be concerned merely with the external conditions of coexistence; rather, it must affect people's hearts and appeal to a new awareness of human dignity. It must be forcefully repeated: Authentic peace is only possible if the dignity of the human person is promoted at every level of society and every individual is given the chance to live in accordance with this dignity. "Any human society, if it is to be well-ordered and productive, must lay down as a foundation this principle, namely, that every human being is a person, that is, his nature is endowed with intelligence and free will. Indeed, precisely because he is a person he has rights and obligations which flow directly and immediately from his very nature. And these rights and obligations are universal, inviolable and inalienable."[1]

The truth about man is the keystone in the resolution of all the problems involved in promoting peace. To teach people this truth is one of the most fruitful and lasting ways to affirm the value of peace.

WOMEN AND THE TEACHING OF PEACE

2. To educate in the ways of peace means to open minds and hearts to embrace the values which Pope John XXIII indicated in the encyclical *Pacem in Terris* as essential to a peaceful society: truth, justice, love, and freedom.[2] This is an educational program which involves every aspect of life and is lifelong. It trains individuals to be responsible for themselves and for others, capable of promoting with boldness and wisdom the welfare of the whole person and of all people, as Pope Paul VI emphasized in the encyclical *Populorum Progressio*.[3] The effectiveness of this education for peace will depend on the extent to which it involves the cooperation of those who in different ways are responsible for education and for the

---

1. Pope John XXIII, encyclical *Pacem in Terris* (April 11, 1963), I:AAS 55 (1963), 259.
2. cf. ibid., 259-264.
3. cf. Pope Paul VI, encyclical *Populorum Progressio* (March 26, 1967)m 14:AAS 59 (1967), 264.

life of society. Time dedicated to education is time truly well spent, because it determines a person's future, and therefore the future of the family and of the whole of society.

In this context, I wish to direct my message for this year's World Day of Peace especially to women and to invite them to become teachers of peace with their whole being and in all their actions. May they be witnesses, messengers, and teachers of peace in relations between individuals and between generations, in the family, in the cultural, social, and political life of nations, and particularly in situations of conflict and war. May they continue to follow the path which leads to peace, a path which many courageous and farsighted women have walked before them!

IN A COMMUNION OF LOVE

3. This invitation to become teachers of peace, directed particularly to women, is based on a realization that to them God "entrusts the human being in a special way."[4] This is not, however, to be understood in an exclusive sense, but rather according to the logic of the complementary roles present in the common vocation to love, which calls men and women to seek peace with one accord and to work together in building it. Indeed, from the very first pages of the Bible God's plan is marvelously expressed: He willed that there should be a relationship of profound communion between man and woman, in a perfect reciprocity of knowledge and of the giving of self.[5] In woman, man finds a partner with whom he can dialogue in complete equality. This desire for dialogue, which was not satisfied

---

4. Pope John Paul II, apostolic letter *Mulieris Dignitatem* (August 15, 1988), 30: AAS 80 (1988), 1725.

5. cf. *Catechism of the Catholic Church*, 371.

by any other living creature, explains the man's spontaneous cry of wonder when the woman, according to the evocative symbolism of the Bible, was created from one of his ribs: "This at last is bone of my bones and flesh of my flesh" (Gn 2:23). This was the first cry of love to resound on the earth!

Even though man and woman are made for each other, this does not mean that God created them incomplete. God "created them to be a communion of persons, in which each can be a 'helpmate' to the other, for they are equal as persons ('bone of my bones') and complementary as masculine and feminine."[6] Reciprocity and complementarity are the two fundamental characteristics of the human couple.

4. Sadly, a long history of sin has disturbed and continues to disturb God's original plan for the couple, for the male and the female, thus standing in the way of its complete fulfillment. We need to return to this plan, to proclaim it forcefully, so that women in particular—who have suffered more from its failure to be fulfilled—can finally give full expression to their womanhood and their dignity.

In our day women have made great strides in this direction, attaining a remarkable degree of self-expression in cultural, social, economic, and political life, as well as, of course, in family life. The journey has been a difficult and complicated one and, at times, not without its share of mistakes. But it has been substantially a positive one, even if it is still unfinished, due to the many obstacles which, in various parts of the world, still prevent women from being acknowledged, respected, and appreciated in their own special dignity.[7] The work of building peace can hardly overlook the need to acknowledge and promote the dignity of women as persons, called to

---

6. ibid., 372.
7. *Mulieris Dignitatem*, 1723.

play a unique role in educating for peace. I urge everyone to reflect on the critical importance of the role of women in the family and in society, and to heed the yearning for peace which they express in words and deeds and, at times of greatest tragedy, by the silent eloquence of their grief.

WOMEN OF PEACE

5. In order to be a teacher of peace, a woman must first of all nurture peace within herself. Inner peace comes from knowing that one is loved by God and from the desire to respond to his love. History is filled with marvelous examples of women who, sustained by this knowledge, have been able successfully to deal with difficult situations of exploitation, discrimination, violence, and war.

Nevertheless, many women, especially as a result of social and cultural conditioning, do not become fully aware of their dignity. Others are victims of a materialistic and hedonistic outlook which views them as mere objects of pleasure and does not hesitate to organize the exploitation of women, even of young girls, into a despicable trade. Special concern needs to be shown for these women, particularly by other women who, thanks to their own upbringing and sensitivity, are able to help them discover their own inner worth and resources. Women need to help women and to find support in the valuable and effective contributions which associations, movements, and groups, many of them of a religious character, have proved capable of making in this regard.

6. In rearing children, mothers have a singularly important role. Through the special relationship uniting a mother and her child, particularly in its earliest years of life, she gives the child that sense of security and trust without which the child would find it difficult to

develop properly its own personal identity and, subsequently, to establish positive and fruitful relationships with others. This primary relationship between mother and child also has a very particular educational significance in the religious sphere, for it can direct the mind and heart of the child to God long before any formal religious education begins.

In this decisive and sensitive task, no mother should be left alone. Children need the presence and care of both parents, who carry out their duty as educators above all through the influence of the way they live. The quality of the relationship between the spouses has profound psychological effects on children and greatly conditions both the way they relate to their surroundings and the other relationships which they will develop throughout life.

This primary education is extremely important. If relationships with parents and other family members are marked by affectionate and positive interaction, children come to learn from their own experience the values which promote peace: love of truth and justice, a sense of responsible freedom, esteem, and respect for others. At the same time, as they grow up in a warm and accepting environment they are able to perceive, reflected in their own family relationships, the love of God himself; this will enable them to mature in a spiritual atmosphere which can foster openness to others and to the gift of self to their neighbor. Education in the ways of peace naturally continues throughout every period of development; it needs particularly to be encouraged during the difficult time of adolescence, when the passage from childhood to adulthood is not without some risks for young people, who are called to make choices which will be decisive for life.

7. Faced with the challenge of education the family becomes "the first and fundamental school of social living,"[8] the first and fundamental school of peace. And so it is not difficult to imagine the tragic consequences which occur when the family experiences profound crises which undermine or even destroy its inner equilibrium. Often, in these circumstances, women are left alone. It is then, however, that they most need to be assisted, not only by the practical solidarity of other families, of communities of a religious nature, and of volunteer groups, but also by the state and by international organizations through appropriate structures of human, social, and economic support which will enable them to meet the needs of their children without being forced to deprive them unduly of their own indispensable presence.

8. Another serious problem is found in places where the intolerable custom still exists of discriminating, from the earliest years, between boys and girls. If, from the very beginning, girls are looked down upon or regarded as inferior, their sense of dignity will be gravely impaired and their healthy development inevitably compromised. Discrimination in childhood will have lifelong effects and will prevent women from fully taking part in the life of society.

In this regard, how can we fail to acknowledge and encourage the invaluable efforts of so many women, including so many congregations of women religious, who on different continents and in every cultural context make the education of girls and women the principal goal of their activity? Similarly, how can we fail to acknowledge with gratitude all those women who have worked and continue to work in providing health services, often in very precarious circumstances,

---

8. Pope John Paul II, apostolic exhortation *Familiaris Consortio* (Nov. 22, 1981), 37:AAS 74 (1982), 127.

and who are frequently responsible for the very survival of great numbers of female children?

WOMEN, TEACHERS OF PEACE IN SOCIETY

9. When women are able fully to share their gifts with the whole community, the very way in which society understands and organizes itself is improved and comes to reflect in a better way the substantial unity of the human family. Here we see the most important condition for the consolidation of authentic peace. The growing presence of women in social, economic, and political life at the local, national, and international levels is thus a very positive development. Women have a full right to become actively involved in all areas of public life, and this right must be affirmed and guaranteed, also, where necessary, through appropriate legislation.

This acknowledgment of the public role of women should not, however, detract from their unique role within the family. Here their contribution to the welfare and progress of society, even if its importance is not sufficiently appreciated, is truly incalculable. In this regard I will continue to ask that more decisive steps be taken in order to recognize and promote this very important reality.

10. With astonishment and concern we are witnessing today a dramatic increase in all kinds of violence. Not just individuals but whole groups seem to have lost any sense of respect for human life. Women and even children are unfortunately among the most frequent victims of this blind violence. We are speaking of outrageous and barbaric behavior which is deeply abhorrent to the human conscience.

We are all called upon to do everything possible to banish from society not only the tragedy of war but also every violation of human rights, beginning with the indisputable right to life, which every person enjoys from the very moment of conception. The violation of the individual human being's right to life contains the seeds of the extreme violence of war. For this reason I appeal to all women ever to take their place on the side of life. At the same time I urge everyone to help women who are suffering, and particularly children, in a special way those scarred by the painful trauma of having lived through war. Only loving and compassionate concern will enable them once again to look to the future with confidence and hope.

11. When my beloved predecessor Pope John XXIII indicated the participation of women in public life as one of the signs of our times, he also stated that, being aware of their dignity, they would no longer tolerate being exploited.[9]

Women have the right to insist that their dignity be respected. At the same time, they have the duty to work for the promotion of the dignity of all persons, men as well as women.

In view of this I express the hope that the many international initiatives planned for 1995—of which some will be devoted specifically to women, such as the conference sponsored by the United Nations in Beijing on work for equality, development and peace— will provide a significant opportunity for making interpersonal and social relationships ever more human, under the banner of peace.

MARY, MODEL OF PEACE

12. Mary, queen of peace, is close to the women of our day because of her motherhood, her example of openness to others' needs, and her witness of suffering. Mary lived with a deep sense of

---

9. cf. *Pacem in Terris*, 1.

responsibility the plan which God willed to carry out in her for the salvation of all humanity. When she was made aware of the miracle which God had worked in her by making her the mother of his incarnate Son, her first thought was to visit her elderly kinswoman Elizabeth in order to help her. That meeting gave Mary the chance to express, in the marvelous canticle of the Magnificat (Lk 1:46-55), her gratitude to God who, with her and through her, had begun a new creation, a new history.

I implore the most holy Virgin Mary to sustain those men and women who, in the service of life, have committed themselves to building peace. With her help may they bear witness before all people, especially those who live in darkness and suffering, and who hunger and thirst for justice, to the loving presence of the God of peace!

The Angelus Reflections, 1995

D uring 1995, in preparation for Beijing, the Holy Father dedicated many of his Sunday Angelus reflections to the role of women in the Church and in society. Several recurrent themes emerge in these short talks: the dignity of women and their equality with men, the role of women as peacemakers, and the contributions of women to the Church and to society. The complete texts of eleven of these talks appear below.

THE FEMININE PRESENCE IN THE FAMILY
(March 19, 1995)

Dear Brothers and Sisters,

1. My pilgrimage today is taking place on the feast of St. Joseph, and naturally my thoughts turn to the world of work marked this year in particular by my meeting with craftsmen. How could we not think, then, of the home in Nazareth where Joseph and Mary helped each other in managing their family and caring for the child Jesus? As a carpenter, Joseph was a craftsman in the truest sense of the term. Mary, who looked after the household chores, could today be considered a housewife and, as such, the model for all those women who are true "homemakers."

2. After a period marked by a certain ideological confusion and pressure, many today are asking that the relationship between

women, the family, and work be dealt with more calmly and objectively, so that the feminine presence in the family can be reevaluated. "Experience confirms," I wrote in the encyclical *Laborem Exercens*, "That there must be a social reevaluation of the mother's role, of the toil connected with it, and of the need that children have for care, love and affection" (no. 19).

In this regard, too, the Family of Nazareth provides a meaningful example: Mary worked at Joseph's side in a personal, feminine manner, which the Gospel accounts allow us to glimpse. Doubtless their harmony was greatly fostered by the husband's trade; Joseph could work close to his family and introduce the young Jesus to his skilled labor as a carpenter.

It is to Mary that we now wish to address our prayer, entrusting to her the hopes and anxieties of every family, especially those at risk from the problems connected with work.

3. O Mary, Mother of Jesus and spouse of Joseph the craftsman, in your heart are gathered the joys and labors of the Holy Family. You offered even your moments of pain to God, always trusting in his Providence. We beg you, protect all women who daily toil so that the domestic community can live in active harmony. Grant that they may be women of Christian wisdom, skilled in prayer and human kindness, strong in hope and affliction, artisans, like you, of authentic peace.

Amen.

CULTURE MUST RESPECT FEMININITY
(June 18, 1995)

Dear Brothers and Sisters,

1. In the course of the Fourth World Conference on Women orga-

nized by the United Nations in Beijing for next September, the international community will be called to reflect on a series of problems concerning the status of women in our time. I would like to express immediately my deep appreciation of this initiative. The theme chosen is in fact extraordinarily important, not only for women, but for the very future of the world which depends so much on the awareness women have of themselves and on the proper recognition which should be guaranteed to them. Therefore, the Church looks hopefully to all that is being done in this regard and considers it a true "sign of the times," as my venerable predecessor John XXIII pointed out in his encyclical, *Pacem in Terris* (no. 22). A "sign of the times" that highlights an aspect of the full truth about the human being which cannot be ignored.

Unfortunately, awareness of the identity and value of women has been obscured in the past—and still is today, in many cases—by various forms of conditioning. Indeed, they have been and are often culpably disregarded and offended by unjust and even violent practices and behavior. All this, on the threshold of the third millennium, is really intolerable! As the Church joins in denouncing all injustices that weigh on women's condition, she intends to proclaim God's plan in a positive way, so that a culture may develop that respects and welcomes "femininity."

2. As I have had more than one occasion to stress, and particularly in the apostolic letter *Mulieris Dignitatem*, the affirmation of woman's dignity must be the basis of this new culture, since she, like man and with man, is a person, that is, a creature made in the image and likeness of God (cf. no. 6), a creature endowed with a subjectivity from which stems her responsible autonomy in leading her own life. This subjectivity, far from isolating people and setting them in opposition, is on the contrary a source of constructive rela-

tionships, and finds its fulfillment in love. Women, no less than men, are fulfilled "in a sincere giving of self" (*Gaudium et Spes*, no. 24). This subjectivity is the basis of a specific way of being for woman, a way of "being feminine," which is enriching and indeed indispensable for harmonious human coexistence, both within the family and in society.

3. May the Blessed Virgin help men and women in our time clearly understand God's plan for femininity. Called to the highest vocation of divine motherhood, Our Lady is the exemplary woman who developed her authentic subjectivity to the full. May Mary obtain for women throughout the world an enlightened and active awareness of their dignity, gifts, and mission.

CULTURE OF EQUALITY IS URGENTLY NEEDED TODAY (June 25, 1995)

Dear Brothers and Sisters,

1. Respect for the full equality of man and woman in every walk of life is one of civilization's great achievements. Women themselves, with their deeply felt and generous daily witness, have contributed to this, as have the organized movements which, especially in our century, have put this subject before world attention.

Unfortunately even today there are situations in which women live, *de facto* if not legally, in a condition of inferiority. It is urgently necessary to cultivate everywhere a culture of equality, which will be lasting and constructive to the extent that it reflects God's plan.

Equality between man and woman is a fact asserted from the first page of the Bible in the stupendous narrative of creation. The Book of Genesis says: "God created man in his own image, in the image of God he created him; male and female he created them"

(Gn 1:27). In these brief lines we see the profound reason for man's grandeur: he bears the image of God imprinted on him! This is true to the same degree for male and female, both marked with the Creator's imprint.

2. This original biblical message is fully expressed in Jesus' words and deeds. In his time women were weighed down by an inherited mentality in which they were deeply discriminated. The Lord's attitude was a "consistent protest against whatever offends the dignity of women" (*Mulieris Dignitatem*, no. 15). Indeed he established a relationship with women which was distinguished by great freedom and friendship. Even if he did not assign the Apostles' role to them, he nevertheless made them the first witnesses of his Resurrection and utilized them in proclaiming and spreading God's kingdom. In his teaching, women truly find "their own subjectivity and dignity" (ibid., no. 14).

In the footprints of her divine Founder, the Church becomes the convinced bearer of this message. If down the centuries some of her children have at times not lived it with the same consistency, this is a reason for deep regret. The gospel message about women, however, has lost none of its timeliness. This is why I wanted to present it once again with all its richness in the apostolic letter *Mulieris Dignitatem*, which I published on the occasion of the Marian Year.

3. One can already perceive the immense dignity of women by the sole fact that God's eternal Son chose, in the fullness of time, to be born of a woman, the Virgin of Nazareth, the mirror and measure of femininity. May Mary herself help men and women to perceive and to live the mystery dwelling within them, by mutually recognizing one another without discrimination as living "images" of God!

COMPLEMENTARITY AND RECIPROCITY
BETWEEN WOMEN AND MEN (July 9, 1995)

Dear Brothers and Sisters,

1. Tomorrow my *Letter to Women* will be published. In it I have wished to address all the women in the world, directly and almost confidentially, to express to them the Church's esteem and gratitude and at the same time to propose once again the main lines of the gospel message concerning them.

Today, continuing the topic I began a few Sundays ago, I wish particularly to reflect on the complementarity and reciprocity which mark the relationship between the persons of the two sexes.

In the biblical account of creation, we read that after creating man God took pity on his loneliness and decided to give him a suitable partner (Gn 2:18). But no creature was able to fill this void. Only when the woman taken from his own body was presented to him, could the man express his deep and joyful amazement, recognizing her as "flesh of [his] flesh and bone of [his] bones" (Gn 2:23).

In the vivid symbolism of this narrative, the difference between the sexes is interpreted in a deeply unitive key: it is, in fact, a question of the one human being who exists in two distinct and complementary forms: the "male" and the "female." Precisely because the woman is different from the man, nevertheless putting herself at the same level, she can really be his "helper." On the other hand, the help is anything but unilateral: the woman is "a helper" for the man, just as the man is a "helper" for the woman!

2. This complementarity and reciprocity emerges in every context of coexistence. "In the 'unity of the two,'" I wrote in my apostolic letter *Mulieris Dignitatem*, "man and woman are called from the beginning not only to exist 'side by side' or 'together,' but they are also called to exist mutually 'one for the other'" (no. 7).

The most intense expression of this reciprocity is found in the spousal encounter in which the man and the woman live a relationship which is strongly marked by biological complementarity, but which at the same time goes far beyond biology. Sexuality in fact reaches the deep structures of the human being, and the nuptial encounter, far from being reduced to the satisfaction of a blind instinct, becomes a language through which the deep union of the two persons, male and female, is expressed. They give themselves to one another and in this intimacy, precisely to express the total and definitive communion of their persons, they make themselves at the same time the responsible coworkers of God in the gift of life.

3. We ask the Blessed Virgin to help us to be aware of the beauty of God's plan. In the special mission entrusted to her, Mary brought all her feminine richness, first to the family of Nazareth and later to the first community of believers. May the men and women of our time learn from her the joy of being fully themselves, establishing mutual relations of respectful and genuine love.

THE VOCATION TO MOTHERHOOD (July 16, 1995)

Dear Brothers and Sisters,

1. Today too, in this splendid place in the mountains, I would like to continue the talks I have been developing over the past few weeks. The fact can never be sufficiently stressed that woman must be appreciated in every area of her life. However, it must be recognized that, among the gifts and tasks proper to her, her vocation to motherhood stands out particularly clearly.

With this gift woman assumes almost a "foundational" role with regard to society. It is a role she shares with her husband but it is indisputable that nature has assigned to her the greater part. I wrote about this in *Mulieris Dignitatem*: "Parenthood—even though it belongs to both—is realized much more fully in the woman, especially in the prenatal period. It is the woman who 'pays' directly for this shared generation, which literally absorbs the energies of her body and soul. It is therefore necessary that the man be fully aware that in their shared parenthood he owes a special debt to the woman" (no. 18).

Woman's singular relationship with human life derives from her vocation to motherhood. Opening herself to motherhood, she feels the life in her womb unfolding and growing. This indescribable experience is a privilege of mothers, but all women have in some way an intuition of it, predisposed as they are to this miraculous gift.

2. The maternal mission is also the basis of a particular responsibility. The mother is appointed guardian of life. It is her task to accept it with care, encouraging the human being's first dialogue with the world, which is carried out precisely in the symbiosis with the mother's body. It is here that the history of every human being begins. Each one of us, retracing this history, cannot fail to reach that moment when he began to exist within his mother's body, with an exclusive and unmistakable plan of life. We were "in" our mother, but without being confused with her: in need of her body and her love, but fully autonomous in our personal identity.

The woman is called to offer the best of herself to the baby growing within her. It is precisely by making herself "gift," that she comes to know herself better and is fulfilled in her femininity. One could say that the fragility of her creature demands the best of her emotional and spiritual resources. It is a real exchange of gifts! The success of this exchange is of inestimable value for the child's serene growth.

3. Mary, whom we invoke today under the title of Our Lady of Mount Carmel, experienced this to the full, having received the task of generating, in time, the eternal Son of God. In her the vocation to motherhood reached the summit of its dignity and potential. May the Blessed Virgin help women to be ever more aware of their mission and encourage the whole of society to express every possible form of gratitude and active closeness to mothers!

THE FEMININE GENIUS (July 23, 1995)

Dear Brothers and Sisters,

1. It is a "sign of the times" that woman's role is increasingly recognized, not only in the family circle, but also in the wider context of all social activities. Without the contribution of women, society is less alive, culture impoverished, and peace less stable. Situations where women are prevented from developing their full potential and from offering the wealth of their gifts should therefore be considered profoundly unjust, not only to women themselves but to society as a whole.

Of course, the employment of women outside the family, especially during the period when they are fulfilling the most delicate tasks of motherhood, must be done with respect for this fundamental duty. However, apart from this requirement, it is necessary to strive convincingly to ensure that the widest possible space is open to women in all areas of culture, economics, politics, and ecclesial life itself, so that all human society is increasingly enriched by the gifts proper to masculinity and femininity.

2. In fact, woman has a genius all her own, which is vitally essential to both society and the Church. It is certainly not a question of comparing woman to man since it is obvious that they have

fundamental dimensions and values in common. However, in man and in woman these acquire different strengths, interests, and emphases and it is this very diversity which becomes a source of enrichment.

In *Mulieris Dignitatem* I highlighted one aspect of feminine genius, that I would like to stress today: woman is endowed with a particular capacity for accepting the human being in his concrete form (cf. no. 18). Even this singular feature which prepares her for motherhood, not only physically but also emotionally and spiritually, is inherent in the plan of God who entrusted the human being to woman in an altogether special way (cf. ibid., no. 30). The woman of course, as much as the man, must take care that her sensitivity does not succumb to the temptation to possessive selfishness, and must put it at the service of authentic love. On these conditions she gives of her best, everywhere adding a touch of generosity, tenderness, and joy of life.

3. Let us look at the Blessed Virgin's example. In the narrative of the wedding at Cana, John's Gospel offers us a vivid detail of her personality when it tells us how, in the busy atmosphere of a wedding feast, she alone realized that the wine was about to run out. And to avoid the spouses' joy becoming embarrassment and awkwardness, she did not hesitate to ask Jesus for his first miracle. This is the "genius" of the woman! May Mary's thoughtful sensitivity, totally feminine and maternal, be the ideal mirror of all true femininity and motherhood!

HISTORY NEEDS TO INCLUDE WOMEN'S CONTRIBUTIONS (July 30, 1995)

Dear Brothers and Sisters,

In the Message which last 26 May [1995] I addressed to Mrs.

Gertrude Mongella, Secretary General of the forthcoming Beijing Conference, I made the observation that because of a new appreciation of woman's role in society, it would be appropriate to rewrite history in a less one-sided way. Unfortunately, a certain way of writing history has paid greater attention to extraordinary and sensational events than to the daily rhythm of life, and the resulting history is almost only concerned with the achievements of men. This tendency should be reversed. "How much still needs to be said and written about man's enormous debt to woman in every other realm of social and cultural progress!" (Address to Gertrude Mongella, no. 6; *L'Osservatore Romano* English edition, May 31, 1995). With the intention of helping to fill this gap, I would like to speak on behalf of the Church and to pay homage to the manifold, immense, although frequently silent, contribution of women in every area of human life.

2. Today in particular, I would like to call to mind woman as teacher. It is an extremely positive fact that in countries where the school system is more developed, the presence of women teachers is constantly increasing. We can of course hope that this greater involvement of women in education will lead to a qualitative leap in the educational process itself. It is a well-founded hope, if one considers the deep meaning of education, which cannot be reduced to the dry imparting of concepts but must aim at the full growth of man in all his dimensions. In this respect, how can we fail to understand the importance of the "feminine genius"? It is also indispensable for the initial education in the family. Its "educational" effect on the child begins when he is still in his mother's womb.

But woman's role in the rest of the formational process is just as important. She has a unique capacity to see the person as an individual, to understand his aspirations and needs with special insight, and she is able to face up to problems with deep involvement. The universal values themselves, which any sound education must always present, are offered by feminine sensitivity in a tone complementary to that of man. Thus the whole educational process will certainly be enriched when men and women work together in training projects and institutions.

3. May the Holy Virgin guide this rediscovery of the feminine mission in the field of education. Mary had a unique relationship with her divine Son: on the one hand she was a docile disciple, meditating on his words in the depths of her heart; on the other, as his mother and teacher, she helped his human nature to grow "in wisdom and in stature, and in favor with God and man" (Lk 2:52). May the women and men who work in the field of education and are committed to building man's future, look to her!

CLOSING THE GAP BETWEEN CULTURAL OPPORTUNITIES FOR MEN AND WOMEN (August 6, 1995)

Dear Brothers and Sisters,

1. Today I would like to introduce our reflection on woman's role, a reflection accompanying us during the weeks of preparation for the Beijing meeting, with a mention of the Servant of God, Paul VI, who died here in Castel Gandolfo exactly 17 years ago.

Speaking of Maria Montessori in 1970, on the occasion of the centenary of her birth, he remarked that the secret of her success, in a certain sense the very origin of her scientific merits, should be sought in her soul or in that spiritual sensitivity and feminine outlook which enabled her to make the "vital discovery" of the child and led her to conceive of an original form of education on this basis (cf. *Insegnamenti di Paolo VI*, VIII [1970], 88).

The name of Montessori is dearly representative of all women who have made important contributions to cultural progress. Unfortunately, in looking objectively at historical reality, we are compelled to notice with regret that even at this level, women have suffered the effects of systematic marginalization. For too long their opportunities for expression outside the family have been denied or restricted, and the women who, despite being thus penalized, succeeded in asserting themselves have had to be very enterprising.

2. It is time, therefore, to close the gap between the cultural opportunities for men and women. I deeply hope that the forthcoming Beijing Conference will provide a decisive impetus in this direction. This will benefit not only women but culture itself, since the vast and variegated world of thought and art has a greater need of their "genius" than ever. Let this not seem a gratuitous assertion! Cultural activity calls into question the human person as a whole, in the twofold complementary sensitivity of man and woman.

This is always important, but especially when the ultimate questions about life are at stake. Who is man? What is his destiny? What is the meaning of life? These decisive questions do not find a satisfactory answer in the laboratories of positive science, but they profoundly challenge men and require, so to speak, a "global thinking" that can harmonize with the sphere of mystery. To this end, how could the contribution of the feminine mind be undervalued? Women's increasingly qualified entrance, not only as beneficiaries but also as protagonists, into the world of culture in all its branches—from philosophy to theology, from the social to the natural sciences, from the figurative arts to music—is a very hopeful sign for humanity.

3. Let us turn our gaze trustingly to the Blessed Virgin. Like the other women of her time, she bore the burden of an age when little

room was allowed them. Yet the Son of God did not hesitate, in some ways, to learn from her! May Mary obtain for all the women in the world a full awareness of their potential and their role at the service of a culture which is ever more truly human and in conformity with God's plan.

EQUAL OPPORTUNITY IN THE WORLD OF WORK (August 20, 1995)

Dear Brothers and Sisters,

1. Doubtless one of the great social changes of our time is the increasing role played by women, also in an executive capacity, in labor and the economy. This process is gradually changing the face of society, and it is legitimate to hope that it will gradually succeed in changing that of the economy itself, giving it a new human inspiration and removing it from the recurring temptation of dull efficiency marked only by the laws of profit. How can we fail to see that, in order to deal satisfactorily with the many problems emerging today, special recourse to the feminine genius is essential? Among other things, I am thinking of the problems of education, leisure time, the quality of life, migration, social services, the elderly, drugs, health care, ecology. "In all these areas a greater presence of women in society will prove most valuable," and "it will force systems to be redesigned in a way which favors the processes of humanization which mark the 'civilization of love'"(*Letter to Women*, no. 4).

2. Nevertheless, it is clear that increasing the role of women in the frequently harsh and demanding structures of economic activity must take into account their temperament and particular needs. Above all, it is necessary to respect the right and duty of woman as mother to carry out her specific tasks in the family, without being

forced by need to take on an additional job. What would society truly gain—even at the economic level—if a short-sighted labor policy were to prejudice the family's endurance and functions?

The safeguarding of this basic good, however, cannot be an alibi with regard to the principle of equal opportunity for men and women also in work outside the family. Flexible and balanced solutions should be found which can harmonize the different needs. In fact— as I wrote in my recent *Letter to Women*—"Much remains to be done to prevent discrimination against those who have chosen to be wives and mothers. As far as personal rights are concerned, there is an urgent need to achieve real equality in every area: equal pay for equal work, protection for working mothers, fairness in career advancements, equality of spouses with regard to family rights and the recognition of everything that is part of the rights, and duties of citizens in a democratic state" (no. 4).

3. Dear brothers and sisters, let us entrust this great challenge of our era to the Blessed Virgin's intercession! Her home in Nazareth was a place of work. Mary, like any good housewife, was busy with domestic tasks while Joseph, with Jesus beside him, worked as a carpenter. May working women look to the hard-working and holy family of Nazareth, and may society be able to find suitable ways to increase their role to the full.

WOMEN IN POLITICAL LIFE (August 27, 1995)

Dear Brothers and Sisters,

1. As the Beijing Conference is now close at hand, today I would like to stress the importance of a greater involvement of women in public life.

A long tradition has seen mostly men involved in politics. Today more and more women are asserting themselves even at the highest levels of representation, national and international.

This process should be encouraged. Politics, in fact, geared as it is to promoting the common good, can only benefit from the complementary gifts of men and women. Of course, it would be naive to expect "miracles" from this alone. It is especially true that for women no less than for men, the quality of politics is measured by the authenticity of the values which inspire them, as well as by the competence, commitment, and moral consistency of those who dedicate themselves to this important service.

In every case women are showing that they can make as skilled a contribution as men, a contribution which indeed is proving particularly significant, especially with regard to the aspects of politics that concern the basic areas of human life.

2. How great, for example, is the role they can play on behalf of peace, precisely by being involved in politics, where the fate of humanity is largely decided.

Dear brothers and sisters, peace is the most pressing need of our time. A collective effort is more than ever necessary to restrain the frenzy of arms. However, peace is not limited to the silence of cannons. It becomes concrete with justice and freedom. It needs a spiritual atmosphere rich in basic elements such as the sense of God, a taste for the beautiful, love for the truth, the option for solidarity, the capacity for tenderness, and the courage of forgiveness. How can we not recognize the valuable contribution which woman can make to promoting this atmosphere of peace!

WOMAN'S ROLE IN THE CHURCH (September 3, 1995)

Dear Brothers and Sisters,

Last Tuesday, as I met the Holy See's Delegation to the Fourth World Conference on Women, which starts in Beijing tomorrow, I confirmed the Church's commitment on behalf of women and I asked the communities and institutions of the Church to make concrete gestures, particularly in service to girls and adolescents, especially the poorest.

Today I appeal to the whole Church community to be willing to foster feminine participation in every way in its internal life.

This is certainly not a new commitment, since it is inspired by the example of Christ himself. Although he chose men as his Apostles—a choice which remains normative for their successors—nevertheless, he also involved women in the cause of his kingdom; indeed, he wanted them to be the first witnesses and heralds of his resurrection. In fact, there are many women who have distinguished themselves in the Church's history by their holiness and hardworking ingenuity. The Church is increasingly aware of the need for enhancing their role. Within the great variety of different and complementary gifts that enrich ecclesial life, many important possibilities are open to them. The 1987 Synod on the Laity expressed precisely this need and asked that "without discrimination women should be participants in the life of the Church, and also in consultation and the process of coming to decisions" (*Propositio* 47; cf. *Christifideles Laici*, no. 51).

2. This is the way to be courageously taken. To a large extent, it is a question of making full use of the ample room for a lay and feminine presence recognized by the Church's law. I am thinking, for example, of theological teaching, the forms of liturgical ministry permitted,

including service at the altar, pastoral and administrative councils, Diocesan Synods and Particular Councils, various ecclesial institutions, curias, and ecclesiastical tribunals, many pastoral activities, including the new forms of participation in the care of parishes when there is a shortage of clergy, except for those tasks that belong properly to the priest. Who can imagine the great advantages to pastoral care and the new beauty that the Church's face will assume, when the feminine genius is fully involved in the various areas of her life?

3. May the Blessed Virgin, model of the Church and ideal of femininity, accompany and sustain the efforts of all the people of goodwill who are involved in the Beijing Conference. May the Mother of the Lord help all humanity to progress in their respect for and promotion of women's true dignity! May she obtain for the Christian community to be ever more faithful to God's plan, following the example of the great women who have embellished its history!

Welcome to Gertrude Mongella, Secretary General of the Fourth World Conference on Women

*I*n May 1995, Pope John Paul II met with Gertrude Mongella *at the Vatican to discuss the Fourth World Conference on Women. Mrs. Mongella, a former official in the Tanzanian government, was secretary general of the conference. The pope gave the following message to her after their meeting.*

May 26, 1995

1. It is with genuine pleasure that I welcome you to the Vatican, at a time when you and your collaborators are engaged in preparing the *United Nations Fourth World Conference on Women*, to be held in Beijing in September. There, the attention of the world community will be focused on important, urgent questions regarding the dignity, the role, and the rights of women. Your visit enables me to express deep appreciation for your efforts to make the Conference, on the theme of "Action for Equality, Development and Peace," the occasion for a serene and objective reflection on these vital goals, and the role of women in achieving them.

The Conference has raised high expectations in large sectors of public opinion. Conscious of what is at stake for the well-being of millions of women around the world, the Holy See, as you are aware, has taken an active part in the preparatory and regional meetings leading up to the Conference. In this process, the Holy See has discussed both local and global issues of particular concern to women not only with other delegations and organizations, but especially with women themselves. The Holy See's delegation, which has itself consisted mostly of women, has heard with keen interest and appreciation the hopes and fears, the concerns and demands of women all over the world.

2. Solutions to the issues and problems raised at the Conference, if they are to be honest and permanent, cannot but be based on *the recognition of the inherent, inalienable dignity of women*, and the importance of women's presence and participation in all aspects of social life. The Conference's success will depend on whether or not it will offer a *true vision of women's dignity and aspirations*, a vision capable of inspiring and sustaining objective and realistic responses to the suffering, struggle, and frustration that continue to be a part of all too many women's lives.

In fact, the recognition of the dignity of every human being is the foundation and support of the concept of *universal human rights*. For believers, that dignity and the rights that stem from it are solidly grounded in the truth of the human being's creation in the image and likeness of God. The United Nations Charter refers to this dignity in the same instance as it acknowledges the equal rights of men and women (cf. Preamble, para. 2), a concept prominent in almost every international human rights instrument. If the potential and aspirations of many of the world's women are not realized, this is due in great part to the fact that their human rights, as acknowledged by these instru-

ments, are not upheld. In this sense, the Conference can sound a
needed warning, and call governments and organizations to work
effectively to ensure the legal guarantee of women's dignity and rights.

3. As most women themselves point out, *equality of dignity* does
not mean "sameness with men." This would only impoverish women
and all of society, by deforming or losing the unique richness and
the inherent value of femininity. In the Church's outlook, women and
men have been called by the Creator to live in profound communion
with one another, with reciprocal knowledge and giving of self, acting together for the common good with the complementary characteristics of that which is feminine and masculine.

At the same time we must not forget that at the personal level
one's dignity is experienced not as a result of the affirmation of
rights on the juridical and international planes, but as the natural
consequence of the concrete material, emotional, and spiritual care
received *in the heart of one's family*. No response to women's issues
can ignore women's role in the family or take lightly the fact that
every new life is *totally entrusted* to the protection and care of the
woman carrying it in her womb (cf. encyclical letter *Evangelium
Vitae*, 58). In order to respect this natural order of things, it is necessary to counter the misconception that the role of motherhood is
oppressive to women, and that a commitment to her family, particularly to her children, prevents a woman from reaching personal fulfil-
ment, and women as a whole from having an influence in society. It
is a disservice not only to children, but also to women and society
itself, when a woman is made to feel guilty for wanting to remain in
the home and nurture and care for her children. A mother's presence
in the family, so critical to the stability and growth of that basic
unity of society, should instead be recognized, applauded, and sup-
ported in every possible way. By the same token society needs to

call husbands and fathers to their family responsibilities, and ought
to strive for a situation in which they will not be forced by economic
circumstances to move away from the home in search of work.

4. Moreover, in today's world, when so many children are facing
crises that threaten not only their long-term development, but also
their very life, it is imperative that the security afforded by responsible parents—mother and father—within the context of the family be
reestablished and reaffirmed. Children need the positive environment of a stable family life that will ensure their development to
human maturity—girls on an equal basis with boys. The Church his-
torically has demonstrated in action, as well as in word, the importance of educating the girl-child and providing her with health care,
particularly where she may not otherwise have had these benefits. In
keeping with the Church's mission and in support of the goals of the
Women's Conference, Catholic institutions and organizations around
the world will be encouraged to continue their care and special
attention to the girl-child.

5. In this year's *World Day of Peace Message*, on the theme of
"Women: teachers of peace," I wrote that the world urgently needs
"to heed the yearning for peace which they [women] express in words
and deeds and, at times of greatest tragedy, by the silent eloquence of
their grief" (1995 *World Day of Peace Message*, no. 4). It should in
fact be clear that "when women are able fully to share their gifts with
the whole community, the very way in which society understands and
organizes itself is improved" (no. 9). This is a recognition of the
unique role which women have in humanizing society and directing it
toward the positive goals of solidarity and peace. It is far from the
Holy See's intentions to try to limit the influence and activity of
women in society. On the contrary, without detracting from their role

in relation to the family, the Church recognizes that women's contribution to the welfare and progress of society is incalculable, and the Church looks to women to do even more to save society from the deadly virus of degradation and violence which is today witnessing a dramatic increase.

There should be no doubt that on the basis of their equal dignity with men "women have a full right to become actively involved in all areas of public life, and this right must be affirmed and guaranteed, also, where necessary, through appropriate legislation" (1995 *World Day of Peace Message*, no. 9). In truth, in some societies, women have made great strides in this direction, being involved in a more decisive way, not without overcoming many obstacles, in cultural, social, economic, and political life (cf. ibid., no. 4). This is a positive and hopeful development which the Beijing Conference can help to consolidate, in particular by calling on all countries to overcome situations which prevent women from being acknowledged, respected, and appreciated in their dignity and competence. Profound changes are needed in the attitudes and organization of society in order to facilitate the participation of women in public life, while at the same time providing for the special obligations of women and of men with regard to their families. In some cases changes also have to be made to render it possible for women to have access to property and to the management of their assets. Nor should the special difficulties and problems faced by single women living alone or those who head families be neglected.

6. In fact, development and progress imply access to resources and opportunities, *equitable access* not only between the least developed, developing, and richer countries, and between social and economic classes, but also *between women and men* (cf. Second Vatican Ecumenical Council, *Constitution on the Church in the Modern*

World, Gaudium et Spes, no. 9). Greater efforts are needed to elimi-
nate discrimination against women in areas that include education,
health care, and employment. Where certain groups or classes are
systematically excluded from these goods, and where communities
or countries lack basic social infrastructures and economic opportunities, women and children are the first to experience marginalization.
And yet, where poverty abounds, or in the face of the devastation
of conflict and war, or the tragedy of migration, forced or otherwise,
it is very often women who maintain the vestiges of human dignity,
defend the family, and preserve cultural and religious values.
History is written almost exclusively as the narrative of men's
achievements, when in fact its better part is most often molded by
women's determined and persevering action for good. Elsewhere I
have written about man's debt to woman in the realm of life and the
defense of life (cf. apostolic letter *Mulieris Dignitatem*, no. 18). How
much still needs to be said and written about man's enormous debt
to woman in every other realm of social and cultural progress! The
Church and human society have been, and continue to be, unmea-
sureably enriched by the unique presence and gifts of women, especially those who have consecrated themselves to the Lord and in
him have given themselves in service to others.

7. The Beijing Conference will undoubtedly draw attention to *the
terrible exploitation of women and girls* which exists in every part of
the world. Public opinion is only beginning to take stock of the
inhuman conditions in which women and children are often forced
to work, especially in less developed areas of the globe, with little or
no recompense, no labor rights, no security. And what about the sexual exploitation of women and children? The trivialization of sexuality, especially in the media, and the acceptance in some societies of
a sexuality without moral restraint and without accountability, are

deleterious above all to women, increasing the challenges that they face in sustaining their personal dignity and their service to life. In a society which follows this path, the temptation to use abortion as a so-called "solution" to the unwanted results of sexual promiscuity and irresponsibility is very strong. And here again it is the woman who bears the heaviest burden: often left alone, or pressured into terminating the life of her child before it is born, she must then bear the burden of her conscience which forever reminds her that she has taken the life of her child (cf. *Mulieris Dignitatem*, no. 14).

A radical solidarity with women requires that the underlying causes which make a child unwanted be addressed. There will never be justice, including equality, development, and peace, for women or for men, unless there is an unfailing determination to respect, protect, love, and serve life—every human life, at every stage and in every situation (cf. *Evangelium Vitae*, nos. 5, 87). It is well known that this is a primary concern of the Holy See, and it will be reflected in the positions taken by the Holy See Delegation at the Beijing Conference.

8. The challenge facing most societies is that of upholding, indeed strengthening, woman's role in the family while at the same time making it possible for her to use all her talents and exercise all her rights in building up society. However, women's greater presence in the work force, in public life, and generally in the decision making processes guiding society, on an equal basis with men, will continue to be problematic as long as the costs continue to burden the private sector. In this area the state has a duty of subsidiarity, to be exercised through suitable legislative and social security initiatives. In the perspective of uncontrolled free-market policies there is little hope that women will be able to overcome the obstacles on their path.

Many challenges face the Beijing Conference. We must hope that the Conference will set a course that avoids the reefs of exaggerated individualism, with its accompanying moral relativism, or—on the opposite side—the reefs of social and cultural conditioning which does not permit women to become aware of their own dignity, with drastic consequences for the proper balance of society and with continuing pain and despair on the part of so many women.

9. Madame Secretary General, it is my hope and prayer that the participants in the Conference will appreciate the importance of what is to be decided there, and its implications for millions of women throughout the world. A great sensitivity is required in order to avoid the risk of prescribing action which will be far removed from the real-life needs and aspirations of women, which the Conference is supposed to serve and promote. With Almighty God's help may you and all involved work with enlightened mind and upright heart so that the goals of equality, development, and peace may be more fully realized.

Letter to Women

T he centerpiece of the Holy Father's 1995 statements about women is his Letter to Women. In it he calls on the Beijing Conference to emphasize the "genius of women" and invites women themselves to reflect on what this means. He notes that the Conference provides an "auspicious occasion" for promoting the many contributions of women—spiritual, cultural, sociopolitical, and economic. The complete text follows.

I greet you all most cordially,
women throughout the world!

June 29, 1995

1. I AM WRITING THIS LETTER to each one of you as a sign of solidarity and gratitude on the eve of the Fourth World Conference on Women, to be held in Beijing this coming September.

Before all else, I wish to express my *deep appreciation* to the United Nations Organization for having sponsored this very significant event. The Church desires for her part to contribute to upholding the dignity, role, and rights of women, not only by the specific work of the Holy See's official Delegation to the Conference in Beijing, but also by speaking directly to the heart and mind of every woman. Recently, when *Mrs. Gertrude Mongella*, the Secretary

General of the Conference, visited me in connection with the Beijing meeting, I gave her a written *Message* which stated some basic points of the Church's teaching with regard to women's issues. That message, apart from the specific circumstances of its origin, was concerned with a broader vision of the situation and problems of *women in general*, in an attempt to promote the *cause* of women in the Church and in today's world. For this reason, I arranged to have it forwarded to every Conference of Bishops, so that it could be circulated as widely as possible.

Taking up the themes I addressed in that document, I would now like to *speak directly to every woman*, to reflect with her on the problems and the prospects of what it means to be a woman in our time. In particular I wish to consider the essential issue of the *dignity* and *rights* of women, as seen in the light of the word of God.

This "dialogue" really needs to begin with a word of thanks. As I wrote in my apostolic letter *Mulieris Dignitatem*, the Church "desires to give thanks to the Most Holy Trinity for the 'mystery of woman' and for every woman—for all that constitutes the eternal measure of her feminine dignity, for the 'great works of God,' which throughout human history have been accomplished in and through her" (no. 31).

2. This word of thanks to the Lord for his mysterious plan regarding the vocation and mission of women in the world is at the same time a concrete and direct word of thanks to women, to every woman, for all that they represent in the life of humanity.

Thank you, *women who are mothers!* You have sheltered human beings within yourselves in a unique experience of joy and travail. This experience makes you become God's own smile upon the newborn child, the one who guides your child's first steps, who helps it to grow, and who is the anchor as the child makes its way along the journey of life.

Thank you, *women who are wives!* You irrevocably join your future to that of your husbands, in a relationship of mutual giving, at the service of love and life.

Thank you, *women who are daughters* and *women who are sisters!* Into the heart of the family, and then of all society, you bring the richness of your sensitivity, your intuitiveness, your generosity and fidelity.

Thank you, *women who work!* You are present and active in every area of life—social, economic, cultural, artistic, and political. In this way you make an indispensable contribution to the growth of a culture which unites reason and feeling, to a model of life ever open to the sense of "mystery," to the establishment of economic and political structures ever more worthy of humanity.

Thank you, *consecrated women!* Following the example of the greatest of women, the Mother of Jesus Christ, the Incarnate Word, you open yourselves with obedience and fidelity to the gift of God's love. You help the Church and all mankind to experience a "spousal" relationship to God, one which magnificently expresses the fellowship which God wishes to establish with his creatures.

Thank you, *every woman*, for the simple fact of being *a woman!* Through the insight which is so much a part of your womanhood you enrich the world's understanding and help to make human relations more honest and authentic.

3. I know of course that simply saying thank you is not enough. Unfortunately, we are heirs to a history which has *conditioned* us to a remarkable extent. In every time and place, this conditioning has been an obstacle to the progress of women. Women's dignity has often been unacknowledged and their prerogatives misrepresented; they have often been relegated to the margins of society and even reduced to servitude. This has prevented women from truly being themselves and it has resulted in a spiritual impoverishment of

humanity. Certainly it is no easy task to assign the blame for this, considering the many kinds of cultural conditioning which down the centuries have shaped ways of thinking and acting. And if objective blame, especially in particular historical contexts, has belonged to not just a few members of the Church, for this I am truly sorry. May this regret be transformed, on the part of the whole Church, into a renewed commitment of fidelity to the Gospel vision. When it comes to setting women free from every kind of exploitation and domination, the Gospel contains an ever relevant message which goes back to the *attitude of Jesus Christ himself.* Transcending the established norms of his own culture, Jesus treated women with openness, respect, acceptance, and tenderness. In this way he honored the dignity which women have always possessed according to God's plan and in his love. As we look to Christ at the end of this Second Millennium, it is natural to ask ourselves: how much of his message has been heard and acted upon?

Yes, it is time to *examine the past with courage*, to assign responsibility where it is due in a review of the long history of humanity. Women have contributed to that history as much as men and, more often than not, they did so in much more difficult conditions. I think particularly of those women who loved culture and art, and devoted their lives to them in spite of the fact that they were frequently at a disadvantage from the start, excluded from equal educational opportunities, underestimated, ignored, and not given credit for their intellectual contributions. Sadly, very little of women's achievements in history can be registered by the science of history. But even though time may have buried the documentary evidence of those achievements, their beneficent influence can be felt as a force which has shaped the lives of successive generations, right up to our own. To this great, immense feminine "tradition" humanity owes a debt which can never be repaid. Yet how many women have been and continue to be valued more for their physical appearance than for their skill, their professionalism, their intellectual abilities, their deep sensitivity; in a word, the very dignity of their being!

4. And what shall we say of the obstacles which in so many parts of the world still keep women from being fully integrated into social, political, and economic life? We need only think of how the gift of motherhood is often penalized rather than rewarded, even though humanity owes its very survival to this gift. Certainly, much remains to be done to prevent discrimination against those who have chosen to be wives and mothers. As far as personal rights are concerned, there is an urgent need to achieve *real equality* in every area: equal pay for equal work, protection for working mothers, fairness in career advancements, equality of spouses with regard to family rights, and the recognition of everything that is part of the rights and duties of citizens in a democratic state.

This is a matter of justice but also of necessity. Women will increasingly play a part in the solution of the serious problems of the future: leisure time, the quality of life, migration, social services, euthanasia, drugs, health care, the ecology, etc. In all these areas a greater presence of women in society will prove most valuable, for it will help to manifest the contradictions present when society is organized solely according to the criteria of efficiency and productivity, and it will force systems to be redesigned in a way which favors the processes of humanization which mark the "civilization of love."

5. Then too, when we look at one of the most sensitive aspects of the situation of women in the world, how can we not mention the long and degrading history, albeit often an "underground" history, of violence against women in the area of sexuality? At the threshold of the Third Millennium we cannot remain indifferent and resigned

before this phenomenon. The time has come to condemn vigorously the types of *sexual violence* which frequently have women for their object and to pass laws which effectively defend them from such violence. Nor can we fail, in the name of the respect due to the human person, to condemn the widespread hedonistic and commercial culture which encourages the systematic exploitation of sexuality and corrupts even very young girls into letting their bodies be used for profit.

In contrast to these sorts of perversion, what great appreciation must be shown to those women who, with a heroic love for the child they have conceived, proceed with a pregnancy resulting from the injustice of rape. Here we are thinking of atrocities perpetrated not only in situations of war, still so common in the world, but also in societies which are blessed by prosperity and peace and yet are often corrupted by a culture of hedonistic permissiveness which aggravates tendencies to aggressive male behavior. In these cases the choice to have an abortion always remains a grave sin. But before being something to blame on the woman, it is a crime for which guilt needs to be attributed to men and to the complicity of the general social environment.

6. My word of thanks to women thus becomes a *heartfelt appeal* that everyone, and in a special way states and international institutions, should make every effort to ensure that women regain full respect for their dignity and role. Here I cannot fail to express my admiration for those women of good will who have devoted their lives to defending the dignity of womanhood by fighting for their basic social, economic, and political rights, demonstrating courageous initiative at a time when this was considered extremely inappropriate, the sign of a lack of femininity, a manifestation of exhibitionism, and even a sin!

In this year's *World Day of Peace Message*, I noted that when one looks at the great process of women's liberation, "the journey has been a difficult and complicated one and, at times, not without its share of mistakes. But it has been substantially a positive one, even if it is still unfinished, due to the many obstacles which, in various parts of the world, still prevent women from being acknowledged, respected, and appreciated in their own special dignity" (no. 4).

This journey must go on! But I am convinced that the secret of making speedy progress in achieving full respect for women and their identity involves more than simply the condemnation of discrimination and injustices, necessary though this may be. Such respect must first and foremost be won through an effective and intelligent *campaign for the promotion of women*, concentrating on all areas of women's life and beginning with a *universal recognition of the dignity of women*. Our ability to recognize this dignity, in spite of historical conditioning, comes from the use of reason itself, which is able to understand the law of God written in the heart of every human being. More than anything else, the word of God enables us to grasp clearly the ultimate *anthropological basis* of the dignity of women, making it evident as a part of God's plan for humanity.

7. Dear sisters, together let us reflect anew on the magnificent passage in Scripture which describes the creation of the human race and which has so much to say about your dignity and mission in the world.

The Book of Genesis speaks of creation in summary fashion, in language which is poetic and symbolic, yet profoundly true: "God created man in his own image, in the image of God he created him; *male and female he created them*" (Gn 1:27). The creative act of God takes place according to a precise plan. First of all, we are told that the human being is created "in the image and likeness of God" (cf. Gn 1:26). This expression immediately makes clear *what is distinct about the human being with regard to the rest of creation.*

We are then told that, from the very beginning, man has been created "male and female" (Gn 1:27). Scripture itself provides the interpretation of this fact: even though man is surrounded by the innumerable creatures of the created world, he realizes that *he is alone* (cf. Gn 2:20). God intervenes in order to help him escape from this situation of solitude: "*It is not good that the man should be alone; I will make him a helper fit for him*" (Gn 2:18). The creation of woman is thus marked from the outset by the *principle of help*: a help which is not one-sided but *mutual*. Woman complements man, just as man complements woman: men and women are *complementary*. Womanhood expresses the "human" as much as manhood does, but in a different and complementary way.

When the Book of Genesis speaks of "help," it is not referring merely to *acting* but also to *being*. Womanhood and manhood are complementary *not only from the physical and psychological points of view*, but also from the *ontological*. It is only through the duality of the "masculine" and the "feminine" that the "human" finds full realization.

8. After creating man male and female, God says to both: "*Fill the earth and subdue it*" (Gn 1:28). Not only does he give them the power to procreate as a means of perpetuating the human species throughout time, *he also gives them the earth, charging them with the responsible use of its resources*. As a rational and free being, man is called to transform the face of the earth. In this task, which is essentially that of culture, *man and woman alike* share equal responsibility from the start. In their fruitful relationship as husband and wife, in their common task of exercising dominion over the earth, woman and man are marked neither by a static and undifferentiated equality nor by an

irreconcilable and inexorably conflictual difference. Their most natural relationship, which corresponds to the plan of God, is the "unity of the two," a relational "uni-duality," which enables each to experience their interpersonal and reciprocal relationship as a gift which enriches and which confers responsibility.

To this "unity of the two" God has entrusted not only the work of procreation and family life, but the creation of history itself. *While the 1994 International Year of the Family* focused attention on *women as mothers*, the Beijing Conference, which has as its theme "Action for Equality, Development and Peace," provides an auspicious occasion for heightening awareness of *the many contributions made by women to the life of whole societies and nations*. This contribution is primarily spiritual and cultural in nature, but sociopolitical and economic as well. The various sectors of society, nations and states, and the progress of all humanity, are certainly deeply indebted to the contribution of women!

9. Progress usually tends to be measured according to the criteria of science and technology. Nor from this point of view has the contribution of women been negligible. Even so, this is not the only measure of progress, nor in fact is it the principal one. Much more important is *the social and ethical dimension*, which deals with human relations and spiritual values. In this area, which often develops in an inconspicuous way beginning with the daily relationships between people, especially within the family, society certainly owes much to the *"genius of women."*

Here I would like to express particular appreciation to those women who are involved in the various *areas of education* extending well beyond the family: nurseries, schools, universities, social service agencies, parishes, associations, and movements. Wherever the work of education is called for, we can note that women are ever ready and willing to give themselves generously to others, especially in serving the weakest and most defenseless. In this work they exhibit a kind of *affective, cultural, and spiritual motherhood* which has inestimable value for the development of individuals and the future of society. At this point how can I fail to mention the witness of so many Catholic women and Religious Congregations of women from every continent who have made education, particularly the education of boys and girls, their principal apostolate? How can I not think with gratitude of all the women who have worked and continue to work in the area of health care, not only in highly organized institutions, but also in very precarious circumstances, in the poorest countries of the world, thus demonstrating a spirit of service which not infrequently borders on martyrdom?

10. It is thus my hope, dear sisters, that you will reflect carefully on what it means to speak of the *"genius of women,"* not only in order to be able to see in this phrase a specific part of God's plan which needs to be accepted and appreciated, but also in order to let this genius be more fully expressed in the life of society as a whole, as well as in the life of the Church. This subject came up frequently during the *Marian Year* and I myself dwelt on it at length in my apostolic letter *Mulieris Dignitatem* (1988). In addition, this year in the Letter which I customarily send to priests for Holy Thursday, I invited them to reread *Mulieris Dignitatem* and reflect on the important roles which women have played in their lives as mothers, sisters, and co-workers in the apostolate. This is another aspect—different from the conjugal aspect, but also important—of that "help" which women, according to the Book of Genesis, are called to give to men.

The Church sees in Mary the highest expression of the "feminine genius" and she finds in her a source of constant inspiration. Mary called herself the "handmaid of the Lord" (Lk 1:38). Through obedience to the Word of God she accepted her lofty yet not easy vocation as wife and mother in the family of Nazareth. Putting herself at God's service, she also put herself at the service of others: *a service of love*. Precisely through this service Mary was able to experience in her life a mysterious, but authentic "reign." It is not by chance that she is invoked as "Queen of heaven and earth." The entire community of believers thus invokes her; many nations and peoples call upon her as their "Queen." *For her, "to reign" is to serve! Her service is "to reign"!*

This is the way in which authority needs to be understood, both in the family and in society and the Church. Each person's fundamental vocation is revealed in this "reigning," for each person has been created in the "image" of the One who is Lord of heaven and earth and called to be his adopted son or daughter in Christ. Man is the only creature on earth "which God willed for its own sake," as the Second Vatican Council teaches; it significantly adds that man "cannot fully find himself except through a sincere gift of self" (*Gaudium et Spes*, 24).

The maternal "reign" of Mary consists in this. She who was, in all her being, a gift for her Son, *has also become a gift for the sons and daughters of the whole human race*, awakening profound trust in those who seek her guidance along the difficult paths of life on the way to their definitive and transcendent destiny. Each one reaches this *final goal* by fidelity to his or her own vocation; this goal provides meaning and direction for the earthly labors of men and women alike.

11. In this perspective of "service"—which, when it is carried out with freedom, reciprocity, and love, expresses the truly "royal" nature of mankind—one can also appreciate that the presence of *a certain diversity of roles* is in no way prejudicial to women, provided

that this diversity is not the result of an arbitrary imposition, but is rather an expression of what is specific to being male and female. This issue also has a particular application within the Church. If Christ—by his free and sovereign choice, clearly attested to by the Gospel and by the Church's constant Tradition—entrusted only to men the task of being an *"icon" of his countenance as "shepherd" and "bridegroom" of the Church through the exercise of the ministerial priesthood*, this in no way detracts from the role of women, or for that matter from the role of the other members of the Church who are not ordained to the sacred ministry, since *all* share equally in the dignity proper to the *"common priesthood"* based on Baptism. These role distinctions should not be viewed in accordance with the criteria of functionality typical in human societies. Rather they must be understood according to the particular criteria of the *sacramental economy*, i.e., the economy of "signs" which God freely chooses in order to become present in the midst of humanity.

Furthermore, precisely in line with this economy of signs, even if apart from the sacramental sphere, there is great significance to that "womanhood" which was lived in such a sublime way by Mary. In fact, there is present in the "womanhood" of a woman who believes, and especially in a woman who is "consecrated," a kind of inherent "prophecy" (cf. *Mulieris Dignitatem*, 29), a powerfully evocative symbolism, a highly significant "iconic character," which finds its full realization in Mary and which also aptly expresses the very essence of the Church as a community consecrated with the integrity of a *"virgin"* heart to become the *"bride"* of Christ and *"mother"* of believers. When we consider the "iconic" complementarity of male and female roles, two of the Church's essential dimensions are seen in a clearer light: the "Marian" principle and the Apostolic Petrine principle (cf. ibid., 27).

On the other hand—as I wrote to priests in this year's Holy

Thursday Letter—the ministerial priesthood, according to Christ's
plan, "is an expression not of domination but of service" (no. 7).
The Church urgently needs, in her daily self-renewal in the light of
the Word of God, to emphasize this fact ever more clearly, both by
developing the spirit of communion and by carefully fostering all
those means of participation which are properly hers, and also by
showing respect for and promoting the diverse personal and commu-
nal charisms which the Spirit of God bestows for the building up of
the Christian community and the service of humanity.

In this vast domain of service, the Church's two-thousand-year
history, for all its historical conditioning, has truly experienced the
"genius of woman"; from the heart of the Church there have
emerged women of the highest calibre who have left an impressive
and beneficial mark in history. I think of the great line of woman
martyrs, saints, and famous mystics. In a particular way I think of
Saint Catherine of Siena and of Saint Teresa of Avila, whom Pope
Paul VI of happy memory granted the title of Doctors of the Church.
And how can we overlook the many women, inspired by faith, who
were responsible for initiatives of extraordinary social importance,
especially in serving the poorest of the poor? The life of the Church
in the Third Millennium will certainly not be lacking in new and
surprising manifestations of "the feminine genius."

12. You can see then, dear sisters, that the Church has many
reasons for hoping that the forthcoming United Nations Conference
in Beijing *will bring out the full truth about women*. Necessary
emphasis should be placed on the *"genius of women,"* not only by
considering great and famous women of the past or present, but also
those *ordinary* women who reveal the gift of their womanhood by
placing themselves at the service of others in their everyday lives.
For in giving themselves to others each day women fulfill their

deepest vocation. Perhaps more than men, women *acknowledge the person*, because they see persons with their hearts. They see them independently of various ideological or political systems. They see others in their greatness and limitations; they try to go out to them and *help them*. In this way the basic plan of the Creator takes flesh in the history of humanity and there is constantly revealed, in the variety of vocations, that *beauty*—not merely physical, but above all spiritual—which God bestowed from the very beginning on all, and in a particular way on women.

While I commend to the Lord in prayer the success of the important meeting in Beijing, I invite *Ecclesial Communities* to make this year an occasion of heartfelt thanksgiving to the Creator and Redeemer of the world for the gift of *this great treasure* which is womanhood. In all its expressions, womanhood is part of the essential heritage of mankind and of the Church herself.

May Mary, Queen of Love, watch over women and their mission in service of humanity, of peace, of the spread of God's Kingdom!

Letter to Mary Ann Glendon and the Holy See's Delegation to the Fourth World Conference on Women

Prior to its departure for Beijing, the Holy Father met with the Holy See's Delegation to the Fourth World Conference, headed by American Professor Mary Ann Glendon. The pope's appeal responds to UN Secretary-General Boutros Boutros-Ghali's request that heads of state make specific commitments to improving the lives of women. The appeal follows.

August 29, 1995

As you prepare to leave for Beijing, I am happy to meet you, the head of the delegation of the Holy See to the Fourth World Conference on Women, and the other members of the delegation. Through you, I extend my best wishes and prayers to the secretary-general of the conference, to the participant nations and organizations, as well as to the authorities of the host country, the People's Republic of China.

My wishes are for the success of this conference in its aim to guarantee all the women of the world "equality, development, and peace," through full respect for their equal dignity and for their inalienable human rights, so that they can make their full contribution to the good of society.

Over the past months, on various occasions I have drawn attention to the positions of the Holy See and to the teaching of the Catholic Church on the dignity, rights, and responsibilities of women in today's society: in the family, in the workplace, in public life. I have drawn inspiration from the life and witness of great women within the Church throughout the centuries who have been pioneers within society as mothers, as workers, as leaders in the social and political fields, in the caring professions, and as thinkers and spiritual leaders.

The secretary-general of the United Nations has asked the participating nations at the Beijing conference to announce concrete commitments for the improvement of the condition of women. Having looked at the various needs of women in today's world, the Holy See wishes to make a specific option regarding such a commitment: an option in favor of girls and young women. Therefore, I call all Catholic caring and educational institutions to adopt a concerted and priority strategy directed to girls and young women, especially to the poorest, over the coming years.

It is disheartening to note that in today's world the simple fact of being a female rather than a male can reduce the likelihood of being born or of surviving childhood; it can mean receiving less-adequate nutrition and health care, and it can increase the chance of remaining illiterate and having only limited access or none at all, even to primary education.

Investment in the care and education of girls as an equal right is a fundamental key to the advancement of women. It is for this reason that today:

- I appeal to all the educational services linked to the Catholic Church to guarantee equal access for girls, to educate boys to a sense of women's dignity and worth, to provide additional possibilities for girls who have suffered disadvantage, and to identify and remedy the reasons which cause girls to drop out of education at an early stage.

- I appeal to those institutions which are involved in health care, especially primary health care, to make improved basic health care and education for girls a hallmark of their service.

- I appeal to the Church's charitable and development organizations to give priority in the allocation of resources and personnel to the special needs of girls.

- I appeal to congregations of religious sisters, in fidelity to the special charism and mission given to them by their founders, to identify and reach out to those girls and young women who are most on the fringes of society, who have suffered most, physically and morally, who have the least opportunity. Their work of healing, caring, and educating and of reaching to the poorest is needed in every part of the world today.

- I appeal to Catholic universities and centers of higher education to ensure that in the preparation of future leaders in society they acquire a special sensitivity to the concerns of young women.

- I appeal to women and women's organizations within the Church and active in society to establish patterns of solidarity so that their leadership and guidance can be put at the service of girls and young women.

As followers of Jesus Christ, who identifies himself with the least among children, we cannot be insensitive to the needs of disadvantaged girls, especially those who are victims of violence and a lack of respect for their dignity.

In the spirit of those great Christian women who have enlightened the life of the Church throughout the centuries and who have often called the Church back to her essential mission and service, I make an appeal to the women of the Church today to assume new forms of leadership in service, and I appeal to all the institutions of the Church to welcome this contribution of women.

I appeal to all men in the Church to undergo, where necessary, a change of heart and to implement as a demand of their faith, a positive vision of women. I ask them to become more and more aware of the disadvantages to which women, and especially girls, have been exposed and to see where the attitude of men, their lack of sensitivity or lack of responsibility, may be at the root.

Once again, through you I wish to express my good wishes to all those who have responsibility for the Beijing conference and to assure them of my support as well as that of the Holy See and the institutions of the Catholic Church for a renewed commitment of all to the good of the world's women.

EXCERPTS OF
RELATED INTEREST
FROM OTHER 1995
PAPAL STATEMENTS

Excerpts from Pope John Paul II's Holy Thursday Letter to Priests

I n 1995, the pope used his annual Letter to Priests to speak about the importance of women in the life of the priest, linking his message to the apostolic letter Mulieris Dignitatem. After discussing the relationship of the priest to women, he reminds priests that women, together with men, "have a part in the prophetic mission of Christ." Priests must guarantee the participation of everyone—men and women alike—in the threefold mission of Christ. Excerpts from the text follow.

April 7, 1995

2. In this letter I wish to reflect on the relationship between priests and women, taking as my point of departure the fact that the subject of women calls for special attention this year just as last year the subject of the family did. In fact the important international conference called by the United Nations in Beijing next September will be devoted to women. This is a new subject with respect to last year's, but closely related to it.

Dear brothers in the priesthood, with this letter I also wish to make reference to another document. Just as in the Holy Thursday message of last year I referred to my letter to families, so this time I would like to redirect your attention to the apostolic letter *Mulieris Dignitatem*, issued on August 15, 1988. As you will recall, this text was prepared at the end of the Marian Year of 1987–1988, during which I published the encyclical *Redemptoris Mater* (March 25, 1987). It is my fervent hope that during this year you will reread *Mulieris Dignitatem*, making it the subject of special meditation and giving particular consideration to its Marian aspects.

A link with the mother of God is fundamental for Christian "thinking." . . . The mother of the Son of God has become the "great inspiration" for individuals and for whole Christian nations. This too, in its own way, tells us much about the importance of women in human life and, in a special way, in the life of the priest.

I have already had occasion to deal with this subject in the encyclical *Redemptoris Mater* and in the apostolic letter *Mulieris Dignitatem*, where I paid homage to those women—mothers, wives, daughters, or sisters—who for their respective sons, husbands, parents and brothers were an effective inspiration for good. Not without reason do we speak of the "feminine genius," and what I have written thus far confirms the validity of this expression. . . .

. . . [A]s we think of the sacrifice of the body and blood, which we offer *in persona Christi*, we find it difficult not to recognize therein the presence of the mother. Mary gave life to the Son of God so that he might offer himself, even as our mothers gave us life, that we too, through the priestly ministry, might offer ourselves in sacrifice together with him. Behind this mission there is the vocation received from God, but there is also hidden the great love of our mothers, just as behind the sacrifice of Christ in the Upper Room there was hidden the ineffable love of his mother. O how truly and yet how discreetly is motherhood and thus womanhood present in the sacrament of holy orders which we celebrate anew each year on Holy Thursday!

4. Christ Jesus is the only son of Mary most holy. We clearly understand the meaning of this mystery; it was fitting that he should be such: A Son so unique by reason of his divinity had to be the only son of his Virgin Mother. But precisely this uniqueness serves in some way as the best "guarantee" of a spiritual "multiplicity." Christ, true man and yet eternal and only begotten Son of the heavenly Father, has, on the spiritual plane, a countless number of brothers and sisters. For the family of God includes everyone: not just those who through baptism become God's adopted children, but in a certain sense all mankind, since Christ has redeemed all men and all women and offered them the possibility of becoming adopted sons and daughters of the eternal Father. Thus have all become brothers and sisters in Christ.

At this point in our reflection on the relationship between priests and women, beside the figure of the mother there emerges the figure of the sister. Thanks to the redemption, the priest shares in a special way in the relationship of brotherhood offered by Christ to all the redeemed.

Many of us priests have sisters in our families. In any event, every priest from childhood onward has met girls, if not in his own family at least in the neighborhood, in childhood games, or at school. A type of mixed community has enormous importance for the formation of the personalities of boys and girls.

Here we encounter the original plan of the Creator, who in the beginning created man "male and female" (cf. Gn 1:27). This divine creative act continues from generation to generation. The Book of Genesis speaks of it in the context of the vocation to marriage: "Therefore a man leaves his father and his mother and cleaves to his wife" (Gn 2:24). The vocation to marriage obviously assumes and requires that the environment in which one lives is made up of both men and women.

In this setting, however, there arise not only vocations to marriage but also vocations to the priesthood and the consecrated life. These do not develop in isolation. Every candidate for the priesthood, when he crosses the threshold of the seminary, has behind him the experience of his own family and of school, where he was able to meet many young people of his own age of both sexes. In order to live as a celibate in a mature and untroubled way it seems particularly important that the priest should develop deep within himself the image of women as sisters. In Christ, men and women are brothers and sisters independent of any bonds of family relationship. This is a universal bond, thanks to which the priest can be open to every new situation, even the most foreign from an ethnic or cultural standpoint, knowing that he must exercise toward the men and women to whom he is sent a ministry of authentic spiritual fatherhood, which gains him "sons" and "daughters" in the Lord (cf. 1 Thes 2:11; Gal 4:19). . . .

6. . . . I would like to touch on the even wider issue of the role which women are called to play in the building up of the Church. The Second Vatican Council fully grasped the logic of the Gospel, in Chapters 2 and 3 of the constitution *Lumen Gentium*, when it presented the Church first as the people of God and only afterward as a hierarchical structure. The Church is first and foremost the people of God, since all her members, men and women alike, share—each in his or her specific way—in the prophetic, priestly, and royal mission of Christ. While I invite you to reread those texts of the council, I will limit myself here to some brief reflections drawn from the Gospel.

Just before his ascension into heaven, Christ commands the apostles, "Go into all the world and preach the Gospel to the whole creation" (Mk 16:15). To preach the Gospel is to carry out the prophetic mission, which has different forms in the Church, according to the charism granted to each individual (cf. Eph 4:11-13). In that circumstance, since it was a question of the apostles and their own particular mission, this task was entrusted to certain men; but if we read the Gospel accounts carefully, especially that of John, we cannot but be struck by the fact that the prophetic mission, considered in all its breadth and diversification, is given to both men and women. Suffice it to mention, for example, the Samaritan woman and her dialogue with Christ at Jacob's well in Sychar (cf. Jn 4:1–42): It is to her, a Samaritan woman and a sinner, that Jesus reveals the depths of the true worship of God, who is concerned not about the place but rather about the attitude of worship "in spirit and truth."

And what shall we say of the sisters of Lazarus, Mary and Martha? The Synoptics, speaking of the "contemplative" Mary, note the preeminence which Christ gives to contemplation over activity (cf. Lk 10:42). Still more important is what St. John writes in the context of the raising of their brother Lazarus. In this case it is to Martha, the more "active" of the two, that Jesus reveals the profound mysteries of his mission: "I am the resurrection and the life; he who believes in me, though he dies, yet shall he live, and whoever lives and believes in me shall never die" (Jn 11:25-26). The paschal mystery is summed up in these words addressed to a woman.

But let us proceed in the Gospel account and enter into the passion narrative. Is it not an incontestable fact that women were the ones closest to Christ along the way of the cross and at the hour of his death? A man, Simon of Cyrene, is forced to carry the cross (cf. Mt 27:32); but many women of Jerusalem spontaneously show him compassion along the *via crucis* (cf. Lk. 23:27). The figure of Veronica, albeit not biblical, expresses well the feelings of the women of Jerusalem along the *via dolorosa*.

Beneath the cross there is only one apostle, John, the son of

Zebedee, whereas there are several women (cf. Mt 27:55-56): the mother of Christ, who according to tradition had followed him on his journey to Calvary; Salome, the mother of the sons of Zebedee, John and James; Mary, the mother of James the Less and Joseph; and Mary Magdalene. All these women were fearless witnesses of Jesus' agony; all were present at the anointing and the laying of his body in the tomb. After his burial, as the day before the Sabbath draws to a close, they depart, but with the intention of returning as soon as it is allowed. And it is they who will be the first to go to the tomb early in the morning on the day after the feast. They will be the first witnesses of the empty tomb, and again they will be the ones to tell the apostles (cf. Jn 20:1-2). Mary Magdalene, lingering at the tomb in tears, is the first to meet the Risen One, who sends her to the apostles as the first herald of his resurrection (cf. Jn 20:11-18). With good reason, therefore, the Easter tradition places Mary Magdalene almost on a par with the apostles, since she was the first to proclaim the truth of the resurrection, followed by the apostles and Christ's disciples.

Thus women too, together with men, have a part in the prophetic mission of Christ. And the same can be said of their sharing in his priestly and royal mission. The universal priesthood of the faithful and the royal dignity belong to both men and women. Most enlightening in this regard is a careful reading of the passages of the First Letter of St. Peter (1 Pt 2:9-10) and of the conciliar constitution *Lumen Gentium* (nos. 10-12; 34-36).

7. In that dogmatic constitution, the chapter on the people of God is followed by the one on the hierarchical structure of the Church. Here reference is made to the ministerial priesthood, to which by the will of Christ only men are admitted. Today in some quarters the fact that women cannot be ordained priests is being

interpreted as a form of discrimination. But is this really the case?

Certainly the question could be put in these terms if the hierarchical priesthood granted a social position of privilege characterized by the exercise of "power." But this is not the case: The ministerial priesthood, in Christ's plan, is an expression not of domination but of service! Anyone who interpreted it as "domination" would certainly be far from the intention of Christ, who in the Upper Room began the Last Supper by washing the feet of the apostles. In this way he strongly emphasized the "ministerial" character of the priesthood which he instituted that very evening. "For the Son of Man came not to be served but to serve, and to give his life as a ransom for many" (Mk 10:45).

Yes, dear brothers, the priesthood which today we recall with such veneration as our special inheritance is a ministerial priesthood! We are at the service of the people of God! We are at the service of its mission! This priesthood of ours must guarantee the participation of everyone—men and women alike—in the threefold prophetic, priestly, and royal mission of Christ. And not only is the sacrament of holy orders ministerial: Above all else the eucharist itself is ministerial. When Christ affirms that "this is my body which is given for you. . . . This cup which is poured out for you is the new covenant in my blood" (Lk 22:19, 20), he reveals his greatest service: the service of the redemption, in which the only begotten and eternal Son of God becomes the servant of man in the fullest and most profound sense. . . .

Excerpts from
Evangelium Vitae (no. 99)

he Holy Father's encyclical letter Evangelium Vitae (The Gospel of Life), *addresses threats to human life in our day: abortion, euthanasia, materialism, excessive individualism, and other practices and attitudes that imperil a "culture of life." He calls especially on women to bear witness to life. An excerpt follows.*

March 25, 1995

99. In transforming culture so that it supports life, *women* occupy a place, in thought and action, which is unique and decisive. It depends on them to promote a "new feminism" which rejects the temptation of imitating models of "male domination," in order to acknowledge and affirm the true genius of women in every aspect of the life of society, and overcome all discrimination, violence, and exploitation.

Making my own the words of the concluding message of the Second Vatican Council, I address to women this urgent appeal: *"Reconcile people with life"* (Closing Messages of the Council, December 8, 1965). You are called to *bear witness to the meaning of genuine love*, of that gift of self and of that acceptance of others which are present in a special way in the relationship of husband and wife, but which ought also to be at the heart of every other interpersonal relationship. The experience of motherhood makes you acutely aware of the other person and, at the same time, confers on you a particular task: "Motherhood involves a special communion with the mystery of life, as it develops in the woman's womb. . . . This unique contact with the new human being developing within her gives rise to an attitude toward human beings, not only toward her own child, but every human being, which profoundly marks the woman's personality" (*Mulieris Dignitatem* no. 18). A mother welcomes and carries in herself another human being, enabling it to grow inside her, giving it room, respecting it in its otherness. Women first learn and then teach others that human relations are authentic if they are open to accepting the other person: a person who is recognized and loved because of the dignity which comes from being a person and not from other considerations, such as usefulness, strength, intelligence, beauty, or health. This is the fundamental contribution which the Church and humanity expect from women. And it is the indispensable prerequisite for an authentic cultural change.

I would now like to say a special word to *women who have had an abortion*. The Church is aware of the many factors which may have influenced your decision, and she does not doubt that in many cases it was a painful and even shattering decision. The wound in your heart may not yet have healed. Certainly what happened was and remains terribly wrong. But do not give in to discouragement and do not lose hope. Try rather to understand what happened and face it honestly. If you have not already done so, give yourselves over with humility and trust to repentance. The Father of mercies is ready to give you his forgiveness and his peace in the Sacrament of Reconciliation. You will come to understand that nothing is definitively lost and you will also be able to ask forgiveness from your child, who is now living in the Lord. With the friendly and expert help and advice of other people, and as a result of your own painful experience, you can be among the most eloquent defenders of everyone's right to life. Through your commitment to life, whether by accepting the birth of other children or by welcoming and caring for those most in need of someone to be close to them, you will become promoters of a new way of looking at human life.

Bibliography

Catechism of the Catholic Church. Washington, D.C.: United States
    Catholic Conference, 1994.

Catholic News Service, *Origins*, 2 vols. (Washington, D.C.: Catholic
    News Service, 1994-1995), 24:466-469, 751-754; 25:186-187.

Flannery, Austin, OP, ed. "Constitution on the Church" (*Lumen
    Gentium*) in *Vatican Council II: The Basic Sixteen Documents*, 1-95.
    Northport, N.Y.: Costello Publishing, 1996.

_____. "Constitution on the Church in the Modern World" (*Gaudium
    et Spes*) in *Vatican Council II: The Basic Sixteen Documents*,
    163-282.

John XXIII. *Peace on Earth* (*Pacem in Terris*). Washington, D.C.:
    United States Catholic Conference, 1963

John Paul II. *The Gospel of Life* (*Evangelium Vitae*). Washington, D.C.:
    United States Catholic Conference, 1995.

_____. *Letter to Women*. Washington, D.C.: United States Catholic
    Conference, 1995.

_____. *Mother of the Redeemer* (*Redemptoris Mater*). Washington,
    D.C.: United States Catholic Conference, 1981.

_____. *On the Dignity and Vocation of Women (Mulieris Dignitatem)*. Washington, D.C.: United States Catholic Conference, 1988.

_____. *On Human Work (Laborem Exercens)*. Washington, D.C.: United States Catholic Conference, 1981.

_____. *The Gospel of Life (Evangelium Vitae)*. Washington, D.C.: United States Catholic Conference, 1995.

_____. *The Vocation and Mission of the Lay Faithful in the Church in the World (Christifidelis Laici)*. Washington, D.C.: United States Catholic Conference, 1988.

National Conference of Catholic Bishops. *Sons and Daughters of the Light: A Pastoral Plan for Ministry with Young Adults*. Washington, D.C.: United States Catholic Conference, 1997.

_____. *Strengthening the Bonds of Peace*. Washington, D.C.: United States Catholic Conference, 1995.

_____. *When I Call for Help*. Washington, D.C.: United States Catholic Conference, 1992.

_____, Ad Hoc Committee for a Pastoral Response to Women's Concerns. *One in Christ Jesus: Toward a Pastoral Response to the Concerns of Women for Church and Society*. Washington, D.C.: United States Catholic Conference, 1992.

_____, Committee on Women in Society and in the Church. *Strengthening the Bonds of Peace: Parish Resource Packet*. Washington, D.C.: United States Catholic Conference, 1996.

Paul VI. *On the Development of Peoples (Populorum Progressio)*. Washington, D.C.: United States Catholic Conference, 1967.

Resources

Strengthening the Bonds of Peace

A Pastoral Reflection on Women in the Church and in Society
This reflection examines leadership in the Church, equality of women and men, and diversity of gifts. The U.S. bishops urge the inclusion of women in church governance through consultation and cooperation in their exercise of authority.
No. 034-6, 16 pp.

Strengthening the Bonds of Peace: Parish Resource Packet

This comprehensive kit is a practical, hands-on resource intended to assist parishes and organizations in encouraging and fostering the participation of women in the Church and in society. Based on the U.S. bishops' pastoral reflection of the same name, the packet provides models for involvement and action and includes a preface and introduction; profiles of women; dimensions of the issue; a prayer service; homily suggestions; four model surveys; sample press materials; proposals for action; a one-day retreat/workshop guide; and a discussion guide and additional resources for continuing the dialogue. From the U.S. bishops' Secretariat for Family, Laity, Women and Youth.
No. 5-018, 51 pp.

Letter to Women

Pope John Paul II prepared this *Letter to Women* as a "sign of solidarity and gratitude" on the eve of the Fourth World Conference on Women, held September 1995 in Beijing. Building on his 1988 apostolic letter *On the*

Dignity and Vocation of Women (Mulieris Dignitatem), the Holy Father extols the "genius of women" and applauds the valuable contributions of all women—mothers, wives, daughters, sisters, those who work, those who are consecrated—as they "enrich the world's understanding and help to make human relations more honest and authentic."
No. 5-052, 20 pp.

My Soul Proclaims (Videotape)
Voices of Catholic Women
This moving one-hour presentation (that originally aired on NBC-TV) captures the historical and contemporary contributions of Catholic women to the Church and society. Among those women in Catholic history featured are Dorothy Day, St. Frances Cabrini, and Blessed Katharine Drexel. Contemporary profiles include Susan Muto, Ph.D., professor of spiritual formation; Sr. Barbara Markey, a creator of the marriage preparation program FOCCUS; Vicki Thorn, founder of Project Rachel; Sr. Cora Billings, a pastoral administrator; and Jeanne Rodriguez, leadership trainer for Hispanic women. Produced by the Catholic Communication Campaign, the video includes a discussion guide and is closed-captioned.
No. 609-3, 60 minutes

To order these resources or to obtain a catalog of other USCC titles, call toll-free 1-800-235-8722. In the Washington metropolitan area or from outside the United States, call 202-722-8716. Visit the U.S. bishops' internet site located at www.nccbuscc.org.